THE
LLAMACORN
COOKBOOK

BARBARA BEERY

Photographs by Natalie Dicks

Illustrations by Elisa Pallmer

GIBBS SMITH
TO ENRICH AND INSPIRE HUMANKIND

First Edition
24 23 22 21 20   5 4 3 2 1

Published by
Gibbs Smith
P.O. Box 667
Layton, Utah 84041

1.800.835.4993 orders
www.gibbs-smith.com

Designed by Mina Bach
Printed and bound in China
Gibbs Smith books are printed on either recycled, 100% post-consumer waste, FSC-certified
papers or on paper produced from sustainable PEFC-certified forest/controlled wood source.
Learn more at www.pefc.org.

Library of Congress Cataloging-in-Publication Data
Names: Beery, Barbara, 1954- author.
Title: The Llamacorn cookbook / Barbara Beery.
Description: First edition. | Layton, Utah : Gibbs Smith, [2020]
Identifiers: LCCN 2019033261 | ISBN 9781423654209 (hardcover) |
ISBN 9781423654216 (epub)
Subjects: LCSH: Snack foods. | LCGFT: Cookbooks.
Classification: LCC TX740 .B4445 2020 | DDC 641.5/3—dc23
LC record available at https://lccn.loc.gov/2019033261

To everyone who believes that an act of kindness can create a rainbow of miracles in us all.

CONTENTS

SWEET TREATS

SAVORY SNACKS

DRINKS

LLAMACORN TREATS TO SHARE

The Llamacorn is the kindest of all the animals in Llamacorn Land, and now he's here to share his fun recipes, and some special recipes from his friends, with you. The one-horned animals in Llamacorn Land enjoy getting together to play, and they love sharing treats and snacks with each other, particularly Llamacorn Cookies (page 16) and Friendship Bread (page 55). They throw the best rainbow parties with Rainbow Cupcakes (page 34) and Rainbow Confetti Parfait (page 52), and they have great picnics with tasty food like Pink-and-White Star Bites (page 68) and Ladybug Cookies (page 22). When they get thirsty from all the fun, they drink Cowicorn Milk (page 79), Laa-Tee-Dah Pink Limeade (page 89), and Cool Breeze Slushies (page 85).

By following the recipes in this cookbook, you can make your favorite foods from Llamacorn Land to share with your family and friends. Be sure to have a parent or another adult with you while cooking and creating in the kitchen, especially for help with knives and hot things. Teamwork always makes cooking go smoothly.

BAKING TIPS

Cupcakes are a beloved treat in Llamacorn Land. Here are some helpful tips and tricks to make, bake, and decorate the perfect cupcake. These hints will also be useful for you when you make some of the tasty cupcakes in the recipe section of this book.

CUPCAKE FLAVORS AND ADDITIONS

* Use any of the three delicious homemade cupcake recipes in this cookbook. You can always use your favorite cake mix to make cupcakes too. These recipes and most boxed cake mixes make 20 to 24 cupcakes.

* Fruit juices work especially well to add a natural sweetness, moistness, and fruit flavor to cupcakes. You can add fruit juice to almost any vanilla or fruit-flavored cupcake recipe by substituting the milk or water called for with an equal amount of fruit juice.

* Make specialty cupcake flavors by folding "stir-ins" into your cupcake batter after it has been mixed. Fun stir-ins include colorful sprinkles, mini chocolate chips, crushed hard candies, marshmallows, or whatever else you think would be good.

CUPCAKE LINERS AND MOLDS

* You can dress up your cupcakes with colorful paper and foil cupcake liners. They are festive and inexpensive, and they make cleanup a snap!

* Bright and colorful silicone cupcake molds are another perfect choice for cupcake liners. Not only do they come in a variety of whimsical shapes, but they are also an eco-friendly baking choice because the molds may be washed and used over and over.

* You can find a large selection of colorful paper cupcake liners and silicone cupcake molds many places online or in the baking sections of craft stores.

* To make sure your baked cup-cakes do not stick to the liners, lightly spray the inside of each liner with nonstick cooking spray before adding the batter.

MEASURE AND MIX

❋ Carefully measure all ingredients. Dry ingredients like flour and sugar should be measured in measuring cups that are specifically made for dry ingredients. Just scoop dry ingredients loosely into measuring cups and level off the top with the back of a table knife. Liquid ingredients like milk and oil should be measured in clear measuring cups with spouts that are specifically made for measuring liquid ingredients. Place the measuring cup on the counter and then bend down and look at the cup at eye level to make sure your measurement is correct.

❋ Bring all ingredients such as eggs, liquids, and butter to room temperature before making your cupcake batter. The ingredients will mix more evenly and the result will be a wonderfully smooth and creamy cupcake batter.

❋ Don't overmix the batter. This will cause the cupcakes to become chewy and tough rather than perfectly moist and tender.

❋ Fill cupcake cups one-half to two-thirds full. Try using an ice cream scoop to fill the cupcake cups—every scoop is the same amount, so each cupcake will be the perfect size every time!

BAKE AND COOL

✳ Always remember to preheat your oven to the correct temperature before putting your cupcakes in to bake. When the oven is ready, gently place the cupcakes inside and then set your timer for the minimum baking time suggested in the recipe.

✳ When the timer goes off, test for doneness by sticking a clean toothpick in the center of a cupcake. If it comes out clean, the cupcakes are ready. If not, let them continue to bake in the oven and set the timer for the additional minutes suggested in the bake time. Then test again.

✳ Make sure you have two 12-cup cupcake pans or one 24-cup cupcake pan available. Having one or the other will ensure you'll have enough room to make one batch of cupcakes. Never put cupcake batter into a warm cupcake pan because the cupcakes will bake unevenly and be lopsided.

✳ For easier and safer handling, put your cupcake pan on a cookie sheet. Bake only one pan of cupcakes at a time and place the pan in the very center of the oven. You can rotate your pan halfway through baking time to ensure that all cupcakes bake and brown evenly.

✳ When cupcakes are done, carefully remove them from the oven using an oven mitt or hot pad. Gently place cupcake pan on a cooling rack for 5 minutes. Remove cupcakes from the pan and then place each cupcake back onto the cooling rack for 30 minutes.

✳ Cupcakes are best eaten the same day they are made—and who doesn't want to eat cupcakes right away? Undecorated cupcakes may be frozen, covered, for up to 3 months.

FROST AND DECORATE

* Before you begin frosting cupcakes, brush the top of each one lightly with your fingers or use a dry pastry brush to remove any loose crumbs.

* Add some fanciful fun to your frosting by adding either a touch or a bunch of color with paste food dyes. Paste food dyes have a much truer and intense color than liquid food dyes. A tiny bit goes a long way in a batch of frosting.

* If you prefer all-natural food dyes, there are several companies that make a complete line of all-natural food dyes and candy decorations.

* To frost cupcakes, spoon a heaping tablespoon of frosting onto the center of each cupcake. Use a table knife, a small plastic picnic knife, or a craft stick to spread and smooth the frosting. Just start in the center and move towards the outer edges of each cupcake. Keep the frosting piled high in the center of the cupcakes. Sometimes, you may even need to add a little more!

* There are endless possibilities for decorating cupcakes! Classic decorations for cupcakes range from colorful decorating sugars, sprinkles, and jimmies to gummy bears, M&M's, Lifesavers, and jelly beans.

* Purchased cookies such as Oreos, vanilla wafers, gingersnaps, animal crackers, and Teddy Grahams work beautifully as cupcake toppers.

* Try pretzel twists or pretzel sticks—plain or dipped in chocolate and decorated with sprinkles.

* Popcorn and miniature marshmallows also make festive choices to top cupcakes.

CUPCAKE RECIPES

The following are some delicious homemade cupcake recipes. The suggested combinations of cupcake flavors, frostings, and decorations used in the themed cupcake recipes in this cookbook are both scrumptious and beautiful. But please feel free to change the cupcake flavors and frostings to best suit the tastes of your family and friends.

Each cupcake recipe calls for self-rising flour and superfine granulated sugar. These ingredients were specifically chosen because they ensure both light and moist cupcakes. If you do not have these items, you can easily transform what you have on hand. Just follow these instructions:

TURN ALL-PURPOSE FLOUR INTO SELF-RISING FLOUR

Add $1^1/2$ teaspoons baking powder and $^1/4$ teaspoon salt to 1 cup all-purpose flour. Combine with a whisk and store in an airtight container.

TURN GRANULATED SUGAR INTO SUPERFINE GRANULATED SUGAR

Place 1 cup granulated sugar into a food processor or blender and whirl for 30 seconds to break down the sugar crystals into smaller ones.

NOTE: Remember to measure the amount of sugar in a recipe *after* you have changed the granulated sugar into superfine granulated sugar.

FAVORITE VANILLA CUPCAKES

 Makes 20 to 24

1¹/₃ cups unsalted butter, room temperature

1¹/₂ cups superfine granulated sugar

6 large eggs, room temperature

2 teaspoons vanilla extract

3 cups self-rising flour

Preheat oven to 350 degrees F. Lightly spray the inside of each cupcake liner or mold with nonstick cooking spray. Set aside.

In a large bowl, cream together the butter and sugar with a hand mixer until light and fluffy.

Beat in eggs, 1 at a time, mixing well after each addition. Stir in vanilla. Add flour, 1 cup at a time, mixing after each addition until just blended.

Fill each liner or mold one-half to two-thirds full of batter. Bake for 15 to 20 minutes.

Carefully remove cupcake pan from oven and place on a cooling rack for 5 minutes. Remove cupcakes from pan and place back on the rack to cool for 30 minutes before frosting and decorating.

CHOCO-LICIOUS CUPCAKES

 Makes 20 to 24

1¹/₂ cups unsalted butter, room temperature

1¹/₂ cups superfine granulated sugar

6 large eggs, room temperature

2 teaspoons vanilla extract

1 teaspoon coconut extract

2 cups self-rising flour

1 cup cocoa powder

2 tablespoons hot water

Preheat oven to 375 degrees F. Lightly spray the inside of each cupcake liner or mold with nonstick cooking spray. Set aside.

In a large bowl, cream together the butter and sugar with a hand mixer until light and fluffy.

Beat in eggs, 1 at a time, mixing well after each addition. Stir in extracts.

In a medium bowl, whisk together the flour and cocoa powder, and then stir into the butter and egg mixture. Add the water and stir together until just blended.

Fill each liner or mold one-half to two-thirds full of batter. Bake for 12 to 15 minutes or until done.

Carefully remove cupcake pan from oven and place on a cooling rack for 5 minutes. Remove cupcakes from pan and place back on the rack to cool for 30 minutes before frosting and decorating.

FRESH STRAWBERRY CUPCAKES

🧁 Makes 20 to 24

1¼ cups unsalted butter, room temperature

½ cup superfine granulated sugar

6 large eggs, room temperature

2 teaspoons vanilla extract

2 teaspoons strawberry extract

½ teaspoon almond extract

3½ cups self-rising flour

½ teaspoon salt

½ cup finely chopped fresh strawberries (about 8 to 10)

Preheat oven to 325 degrees F. Lightly spray the inside of each cupcake liner or mold with nonstick cooking spray. Set aside.

In a large bowl, cream together the butter and sugar with a hand mixer until light and fluffy.

Beat in eggs, 1 at a time, mixing well after each addition. Stir in extracts.

In a medium bowl, whisk together the flour and salt, and then stir into the butter and egg mixture. Fold in strawberries.

Fill each liner or mold one-half to two-thirds full of batter. Bake for 20 to 25 minutes.

Carefully remove cupcake pan from oven and place on a cooling rack for 5 minutes. Remove cupcakes from pan and place back on the rack to cool for 30 minutes before frosting and decorating.

FROSTING RECIPES

Each frosting recipe should make enough to frost 24 cupcakes.

BUTTERCREAM FROSTING

- 4 cups powdered sugar, or more if needed
- Pinch of salt
- 1/4 to 1/2 cup half-and-half or whole milk
- 1/2 cup unsalted butter, room temperature
- 1 teaspoon vanilla extract
- 1/2 teaspoon almond, coconut, strawberry, or raspberry extract (optional)
- Paste food coloring (optional)

Place powdered sugar and salt in a large bowl and mix with a whisk to break apart any lumps.

Add half-and-half or milk and slowly mix with a hand mixer on low. Add butter and turn the mixer to high speed. Beat until fluffy. You may need to add a little more milk if the mixture is too thick or a little more powdered sugar if the mixture is too thin.

Turn hand mixer to low. Beat in vanilla and additional extracts or food coloring if using.

CHOCOLATE BUTTER-CREAM FROSTING

Follow the recipe for Buttercream Frosting, but add 1/4 cup cocoa powder to the dry ingredients.

MERINGUE BUTTER-CREAM FROSTING

Follow the recipe for Buttercream Frosting, but add 1 tablespoon meringue powder to the dry ingredients. If you're not going to use this frosting right away, keep it at room temperature, covered, to prevent it from developing a dry crust on top. Store any leftover frosting, covered, in the freezer for up to one month or in the refrigerator for up to one week.

Now that you know some great tips and hints for baking, what are you going to make first?

LLAMACORN COOKIES

🧁 Makes 12 (4-inch) cookies

1/2 cup butter or margarine, softened

3/4 cup sugar

1 egg

1/2 teaspoon almond extract

1 tablespoon maraschino cherry juice or syrup (optional)

1 to 2 drops pink gel food coloring (optional)

2 cups all-purpose flour

1/2 teaspoon baking soda

1/2 teaspoon salt

Llama-shaped cookie cutter

Preheat oven to 375 degrees F.

Cream butter or margarine in a large mixing bowl. Add sugar and beat until light and fluffy. Add egg and almond extract. If you would like for your cookies to be pink, add in the maraschino cherry juice or syrup and pink gel food coloring with the egg and almond extract.

Combine flour, baking soda, and salt in a separate bowl. Add to creamed mixture and blend well.

Flatten out dough until it is about 1/4 inch thick, cover with plastic wrap, and put in the freezer for 15 minutes to chill.

Divide dough in half. Roll to 1/8 inch thick on a lightly floured work area. Cut out with a llama-shaped cookie cutter. Place cookies, 1 inch apart, on cookie sheets sprayed with nonstick cooking spray. Bake for 8 to 10 minutes or until lightly browned. Let cookies cool on cookie sheets for 5 minutes then carefully remove. Let cool completely before frosting and decorating.

To make the frosting, combine meringue powder, powdered sugar, water, and vanilla and almond extracts in a mixing bowl.

Beat on high speed with an electric mixer for 3 to 5 minutes.

Divide frosting between 2 bowls. Add red and pink food coloring to 1 bowl to get a dark pink color. Add a small drop of pink food coloring to the other bowl to get a light pink color.

Decorator frosting

   3 tablespoons commercial
     meringue powder

   2 cups powdered sugar

   $1/4$ cup plus 2 tablespoons
     warm water

   1 teaspoon vanilla extract

   $1/2$ teaspoon almond extract

   Red gel food coloring

   Pink gel food coloring

   Pink sanding sugar

   Candy unicorn horns

   Pink jimmies

   Black gel food coloring

Using the photo as your guide, use a knife to spread dark pink frosting onto the head and ears of the llamacorn. Then frost the tail and legs.

Place the light pink frosting into a ziplock bag and cut the tip off. Lightly squeezing the bag, swirl frosting onto the body of the llamacorn to make his fur. Sprinkle pink sanding sugar over top. Then use the bag of frosting to pipe the hair on the top of the head. Insert candy unicorn horn. Sprinkle pink jimmies over top. Carefully add the eyebrows, face, and feet.

Place the remaining dark pink frosting into a ziplock bag with the tip cut off. Pipe wave design onto the llamacorn's body then add the cheeks and details on the ears.

Combine remaining frosting into a small mixing bowl. Add black food coloring to get desired color.

Place the black frosting into a ziplock bag and cut a very small portion of the tip off. Pipe the eyes, nose, and mouth. Let cookies dry for 20 minutes before serving.

PRETTY PARTY PUFFS

 Makes 18 to 24 cookies

3 egg whites

3/4 cup sugar

1/4 teaspoon cream of tartar

1/2 teaspoon vanilla or almond extract

2 to 3 drops pink gel food coloring

Confetti sprinkles, silver decorating balls, or pink sugar crystals

Preheat oven to 250 degrees F. Line 2 cookie sheets with aluminum foil.

In a large bowl, whip egg whites with electric mixer until soft peaks form. With mixer on, slowly add sugar, 1 tablespoon at a time. Add cream of tartar, vanilla or almond extract, and gel food coloring. Continue beating until stiff peaks form.

Spoon mounds (about 2 tablespoons each) onto foil-lined cookie sheets; space them about 1/2 inch apart. Sprinkle with decoration of choice.

Place both cookie sheets on the middle rack of the preheated oven and bake for 1 hour. Then turn off oven and leave oven door closed for 10 minutes.

Remove puffs from baking sheets and store in an airtight container.

LLAMACORN'S MERINGUE COOKIES

Makes 18 to 24 cookies

3 egg whites, room temperature

¾ cup sugar

¼ teaspoon cream of tartar

¼ teaspoon vanilla or almond extract

½ cup confetti sprinkles, divided

Preheat oven to 250 degrees F. Line 2 cookie sheets with aluminum foil.

In a large bowl, whip egg whites with a mixer until soft peaks form. With mixer running, slowly add sugar, 1 tablespoon at a time. Add cream of tartar and vanilla or almond extract. Continue beating until stiff peaks form. Fold in ¼ cup confetti sprinkles.

Spoon mounds (about 2 tablespoons each) about ½ inch apart onto foil-lined cookie sheets. Sprinkle each cookie evenly with the remaining confetti sprinkles.

Place both cookie sheets on the middle rack of the oven and bake for 1 hour. Turn off oven and leave oven door closed for another 10 minutes. Remove cookies from oven. Cool on cookie sheets for 10 minutes then store in an airtight container until ready to serve.

LADYBUG COOKIES

🧁 Makes 24 little ladybugs

24 vanilla wafer cookies

1 (16-ounce) container creamy vanilla frosting

Red paste food coloring

1/2 cup chocolate chip mini morsels

24 Milk Duds or Junior Mints

Place cookies on a large cookie sheet that has been lined with aluminum foil. Place the frosting in a small bowl and add red paste food coloring. Mix well.

Spread about 1/2 teaspoon of frosting on the rounded side of each vanilla wafer.

Position 5 to 7 mini morsels on the top of each frosted cookie to create the ladybug's spots. Place a small amount of frosting on a Milk Dud or Junior Mint and secure it to a frosted cookie at the top edge to make the ladybug's head. Repeat for all cookies.

Place entire cookie sheet with decorated cookies in the refrigerator and chill for 10 minutes, or until ready to serve.

MYSTICAL
MOON PIES

 Makes 12 pies

1 (7-ounce) jar marshmallow crème

Assorted food coloring

24 chocolate wafer cookies, non-filled

Assorted candy decorations and sprinkles

Put $^1/_2$ cup marshmallow crème in each of 3 different bowls. Add a different food coloring to each bowl and stir to blend. Or you can leave the crème uncolored if you prefer.

Take a wafer cookie and place about $^1/_2$ teaspoon marshmallow crème on top. Place another matching wafer on top. The rounded side of the wafer should be placed on top of the marshmallow crème. Repeat process to make 12 pies.

Place a dollop of marshmallow crème on top cookie of each pie. Experiment and have fun with different color combinations, or different size cookie stacks.

Garnish the top of each moon pie with candy decorations of your choice. Serve immediately.

BUTTERFLY MASKS

Makes 8 to 10 cookie masks

¹/₄ cup flour, plus 2 tablespoons for work area

¹/₄ cup powdered sugar

1 roll refrigerated sugar cookie dough

Small pretzels

1 (16-ounce) container creamy vanilla frosting

Assorted sugar sprinkles, jimmies, and colorful small candies

Preheat oven to 350 degrees F.

Line a cookie sheet with aluminum foil and spray with nonstick cooking spray.

In a large bowl, knead ¹/₄ cup flour and powdered sugar into cookie dough. Cover and refrigerate for 10 minutes.

Dust work area with remaining 2 tablespoons of flour and roll out dough about ¹/₂ inch thick. Using a 2 to 3-inch heart-shaped cookie cutter, cut out 2 hearts per mask. Lay hearts on cookie sheet overlapping the pointed ends of each heart and press down slightly to shape the dough into one piece.

Insert small pretzels pieces into the dough (as shown in photograph) to form the butterfly's antennae.

Using a very small cookie cutter, or with the tip of a butter knife, cut out oval-shaped circles in center of each heart for the eyes.

Bake cookies for 12 minutes.

Remove from oven and cool 10 minutes. Then frost and decorate with assorted candies.

ICE CREAM SUNDAE CUPCAKE CONES

🧁 Makes 24 cupcakes

24 flat-bottomed ice cream cones

Fresh Strawberry Cupcakes (page 14)

1 quart vanilla ice cream

1 bottle "Magic Shell" chocolate coating

Rainbow sprinkles

1 (8-ounce) bottle maraschino cherries with stems

Place 2 muffin pans on cookie sheets. Stand ice cream cones in muffin cups and set aside.

Make cupcake batter according to directions. Fill each prepared ice cream cone one-half to two-thirds full and then bake as directed in recipe. Cool cupcakes in pan for at least 1 hour.

When ready to serve, top each cupcake cone with a scoop of ice cream. Top with chocolate coating, sprinkles, and a cherry. Serve immediately.

BEARICORN'S S'MORE CUPCAKES

🧁 Makes 24 cupcakes

Choco-licious Cupcakes
(page 13)

Chocolate Buttercream
Frosting (page 15)

2 cups mini marshmallows

1 box Teddy Grahams

Small kitchen torch
(optional)

Make cupcakes according to directions; cool.

Make frosting according to directions and frost cooled cupcakes. Add a layer of mini marshmallows around the edge of each cupcake. Pipe chocolate frosting around the upper edge of the marshmallows. Insert 6 or 7 Teddy Grahams, facing outward, to make a teddy bear "crown" on top of the cupcake. Add a few more marshmallows in the center of the teddy bear crown.

With an adult helper, carefully toast the edges of your mini marshmallows, if desired, using a small kitchen torch. Serve immediately.

TiGERCORN'S WiLD CUPCAKES

Makes 24 cupcakes

Choco-licious Cupcakes
(page 13)

1 (16-ounce) container vanilla
frosting

Orange paste food coloring

Black and brown tubes of
decorator's frosting

Make cupcakes according to directions, using animal print cupcake liners.

Divide the frosting between 2 bowls. Add the orange food coloring to 1 bowl and mix well. Frost cooled cupcakes with white or orange frosting. Use decorator's frosting to make zebra, leopard, and tiger patterns on cupcakes.

RAINBOW CUPCAKES

 Makes 24 cupcakes

Favorite Vanilla Cupcakes
(page 13)

Purple, blue, green, yellow,
orange, and red paste
food coloring

Meringue Buttercream
Frosting (page 15)

Decorating sprinkles

Make cupcake batter according to directions. Divide batter into 6 small bowls and tint each bowl with 1 of the paste food colorings.

Place a dollop of each colored batter into each prepared cupcake mold or liner in the following order: purple, blue, green, yellow, orange, and red. With a wooden skewer, draw a "figure 8" in the batter of each cupcake to swirl the colors. Bake and cool.

Make frosting according to directions. Divide frosting among 6 small bowls and tint each bowl with 1 of the paste food colorings. Keep the bowls of frosting covered when not using so it stays spreadable.

Place each frosting color in separate ziplock bags and seal shut. Snip 1 bottom corner off each bag with kitchen scissors. Frost 4 cupcakes with purple, 4 cupcakes with blue, 4 with green, and so on until you have used all 6 colors and all the cupcakes are frosted. Decorate with sprinkles.

GIRAFFICORN'S CLOUD CAKES

 Makes 24 cupcakes

1 box angel food cake mix

1 teaspoon vanilla extract

1/2 teaspoon almond extract

1/4 cup confetti sprinkles

2 to 3 cups whipped cream or whipped topping

1 cup flaked coconut

Preheat oven to 350 degrees F.

Make cake mix according to package directions, adding vanilla and almond extract. Mix on low speed for about 1 minute then mix on medium for 1 more minute.

Fold in confetti sprinkles.

Line 2 cupcake pans with foil cupcake liners. Spoon batter into each cup, filling three-fourths full. Bake about 25 minutes or until the tops are dark golden brown.

Carefully remove cupcakes from oven and cool in pan 5 minutes. Remove from cupcake pans and cool at least 1 hour before frosting.

Frost with "clouds" of whipped cream on each cupcake and sprinkle with coconut.

COTTON CANDY CUPCAKES

🧁 Makes 24 cupcakes

1 box strawberry or white cake mix

Milk

$1/2$ teaspoon vanilla extract

Pink gel food coloring

1 (16-ounce) container vanilla frosting

2 bags pink cotton candy

Preheat oven to 350 degrees F.

Make cake mix according to package directions, substituting milk for water and adding vanilla.

Line 2 cupcake pans with pink paper cupcake liners. Divide batter evenly between liners. Bake according to package directions.

Cool cupcakes 10 to 15 minutes.

Meanwhile, in a medium bowl, stir 1 to 2 drops of pink gel food coloring into frosting. Mix well. Then frost cupcakes.

Divide cotton candy into 24 small sections and set each one on top of a frosted cupcake.

POPCORN CUPCAKES

Makes 24 cupcakes

1 box white cake mix

Milk

1 teaspoon vanilla extract

$1/2$ teaspoon almond extract

4 cups popped popcorn

1 (16-ounce) container vanilla frosting

1 cup white chocolate chips

Preheat oven to 350 degrees F.

Make cake mix according to package directions, but substitute milk for water. Add vanilla and almond extracts to the batter and stir to blend.

Line 2 cupcake pans with paper liners and spray generously with nonstick cooking spray.

Divide batter evenly between 24 muffin cups using an ice cream scoop to keep the amount of batter equal between cups. Bake and cool according to package directions.

Fill a large bowl with the popcorn.

Frost each cupcake generously with frosting and then dip each frosted cupcake into the popcorn.

Add white chocolate chips to fill in the spots where popcorn did not stick to the frosting.

LITTLE LOLLIPOP CAKES

Makes 24 cupcakes

Choco-licious Cupcakes
(page 13)

Buttercream Frosting
(page 15)

Assorted candies

Whimsical lollipops

Make cupcakes according to directions; cool.

Make frosting according to directions.

Frost cupcakes and decorate with candies. Insert lollipops into each cupcake.

Pink Pudding

Makes 4 servings

1 small package vanilla instant pudding mix

1 teaspoon vanilla extract

Pink gel food coloring

Decorating sugars or sprinkles (optional)

Raspberries, maraschino cherries, or sliced strawberries (optional)

Make pudding in a mixing bowl according to package directions, adding in the vanilla. Stir in 1 to 2 drops pink gel food coloring.

Chill and serve with optional garnishes as desired.

43

ENCHANTED UNICORN HORNS

 Makes 10 to 12
unicorn horns

8 to 10 squares vanilla candy
coating or almond bark

10 to 12 waffle or wafer-
type ice cream cones with
pointed ends

Assorted decorating
sprinkles, placed in small
saucers

Ice cream, frozen yogurt, or
fruit sorbet

Melt vanilla candy coating or almond bark according
to package directions.

Place melted candy coating in a medium-size bowl. Dip
about $1^1/_2$ to 2 inches of each cone (the big, open end)
into melted candy coating.

Now take each dipped "unicorn horn" and dip the
candy-covered end into decorating sprinkles.

Place each finished unicorn horn carefully on an
aluminum foil–lined cookie sheet sprayed with nonstick cooking spray. Place in freezer 5 to 10 minutes
to harden coating.

Remove unicorn horns from freezer. Fill each one with
ice cream, frozen yogurt, or sorbet. Top with candy or
additional sprinkles if desired.

CANDY-COATED DRAGONFLIES

Makes 8 dragonflies

8 to 10 squares vanilla candy coating or almond bark

Powdered food coloring* (optional)

8 (8-inch) pretzel rods

16 large pretzel twists

Assorted decorating sugars or sprinkles

Melt candy coating according to package directions. Remove from heat and pour into 2 or 3 small bowls. You may add 2 to 4 drops of food coloring to each bowl. Stir to blend color.

Place pretzel rods on an aluminum foil–lined cookie sheet sprayed with nonstick cooking spray (about 3 inches apart from each other). These are the dragon-flies' long bodies.

Carefully spoon the warm melted candy coating over each pretzel rod to cover completely.

Dip each pretzel twist in the candy coating and place 1 on each side of the upper half of the pretzel rods. The pretzel twists should rest on top of the pretzel rods and just barely touch one another. These form the dragonflies' wings.

Sprinkle each dragonfly pretzel with decorating sugars or sprinkles.

Place cookie sheet in freezer for 5 to 10 minutes to allow candy coating to harden.

Remove from freezer and carefully take each drag-onfly off cookie sheet to serve.

*Liquid and paste food colorings cause melted candy coating and chocolate to "seize." This means when it is added to the melted ingredient, it makes it clump together and become lumpy and stiff. Powdered food coloring may be found in craft or cake decorat-ing stores.

CRISPY ICE CREAM SANDWICHES

 Makes 12 ice cream sandwiches

¹/₄ cup butter or margarine (do not use soft-spread margarine)

1 (10-ounce) bag marshmallows

1 teaspoon vanilla extract

6 cups crispy rice cereal

¹/₂ cup decorating sprinkles (optional)

Ice cream

Spray a large saucepan with nonstick cooking spray. Melt butter or margarine with marshmallows in pan, stirring often. Stir in vanilla. Add cereal and remove from heat.

Stir together until a large ball begins to form. Add decorating sprinkles, if desired.

Scoop mix into a 9 x 13-inch pan that has been sprayed with nonstick cooking spray and flatten evenly. Chill in the refrigerator for 10 minutes. Remove from refrigerator and cut into 2-inch squares.

Put a small scoop of ice cream on top of 1 square and top with another square. Trim off extra ice cream so it is square. Press together and eat right away, or place in freezer until ready to serve.

BAKED SNOWFLAKES

🧁 Makes 10 snowflakes

10 fajita-size flour tortillas, room temperature

1 tablespoon butter, melted

Blue colored sugar

1/2 cup powdered sugar

Preheat the oven to 350 degrees F.

Fold each tortilla into quarters and then snip out shapes with clean kitchen scissors as if you were making a paper snowflake. If your tortillas are stiff, soften them in the microwave for 15 seconds.

Place the snowflakes on an aluminum foil–lined cookie sheet, brush lightly with melted butter, and sprinkle each one with blue sugar.

Bake 5 to 7 minutes or until the edges are very lightly browned. Remove from the oven and cool 5 minutes.

Dust with powdered sugar and serve.

RAINBOW CONFETTI PARFAIT

Makes 4 to 6 parfaits

1/2 cup sugar

3 tablespoons cornstarch

1/4 teaspoon salt

2 cups milk

1 teaspoon vanilla extract

1 tablespoon butter

Pink, green, and yellow food coloring

Whipped cream and rainbow sprinkles for garnish

Colored mini marshmallows for garnish, optional

In a small bowl, combine sugar, cornstarch, and salt.

In a medium saucepan over medium heat, warm milk until bubbles form around the edges.

Pour sugar mixture into hot milk, a little at a time, stirring to dissolve. Continue to cook and stir until mixture thickens enough to coat the back of a metal spoon. Do not boil.

Remove from heat and add in vanilla and butter; stir until butter melts. Divide pudding into thirds and tint each portion with a different food coloring. Color 1 pink, 1 green, and 1 yellow.

Divide evenly among 4 to 6 parfait glasses, layering each pudding color. Cover and chill at least 2 hours before serving.

Garnish with a dollop of whipped cream, rainbow sprinkles, and mini marshmallows, if desired.

FRIENDSHIP BREAD

 Makes 8 servings

Bread

1 (8-count) can refrigerated buttermilk biscuits

4 tablespoons sugar

4 tablespoons brown sugar

1 teaspoon cinnamon

4 tablespoons butter, melted

Icing

$1/2$ cup powdered sugar

Tiny pinch of salt

$1/4$ teaspoon vanilla extract

1 teaspoon milk

Candy sprinkles, optional

Preheat oven to 350 degrees F.

Cut each biscuit into 4 equal pieces.

Mix together sugars and cinnamon in a large ziplock bag. Drop 5 to 7 biscuit pieces into the mixture, seal the bag shut, and shake. Repeat until all the pieces are coated.

Spray 8 silicone or paper muffin cup liners with non-stick cooking spray and place on a cookie sheet. Drop 4 to 6 coated biscuit pieces into each cup. Sprinkle with any remaining sugar mixture and then drizzle with melted butter.

Carefully place in the oven, and bake 10 to 12 minutes.

Remove from oven; cool slightly for a few minutes. Set aside.

To make the icing, combine the powdered sugar, salt, vanilla and milk; stir to blend. The icing should be runny. Take a spoonful and drizzle over each piece of Friendship Bread. Decorate with candy sprinkles if desired.

FLAMINGOCORN'S FAVORITE STRAWBERRIES

 Makes 12 strawberries

8 ounces cream cheese, room temperature

1 teaspoon vanilla extract

3 to 4 tablespoons powdered sugar

1 to 2 drops red food coloring

12 strawberries, tops and bottoms slightly trimmed

2 tablespoons rainbow sprinkles

Combine cream cheese, vanilla, powdered sugar, and food coloring in a small mixing bowl. Using a hand mixer, beat 2 to 3 minutes until mixture is light and fluffy.

Use a small melon baller to scoop out tops of each strawberry.

Fill a small ziplock bag with the cream cheese mixture. Snip off 1 lower corner of the bag with a pair of kitchen scissors. Squeeze air out of bag and securely seal shut.

Generously pipe the cream cheese filling from the bag into the hole of each strawberry, making a swirl to finish off each.

Decorate with sprinkles and serve immediately. Strawberries may also be covered and stored up to 4 hours. If storing, decorate with sprinkles right before serving.

SPARKLY BAGEL CRISPS

 Makes 24 crisps

6 mini bagels

1/2 cup mixed colored sugars

1 teaspoon cinnamon

1 tablespoon butter, softened

Preheat oven to 325 degrees F. Line a cookie sheet with aluminum foil and spray with nonstick cooking spray. Set aside.

Have an adult assistant help you slice the bagels in half, and then slice each piece in half again to make thin circles.

Combine sugar and cinnamon in a measuring cup. Stir to blend. Set aside.

With a small spatula or pastry brush, coat 1 side of each bagel slice with butter and sprinkle evenly with sugar mixture.

Place bagel slices on prepared cookie sheet and bake for 15 to 20 minutes, or until lightly browned. Remove from oven. Cool on pan for 5 minutes. Remove from pan and place on cooling rack for 10 minutes. The chips will become crispier as they cool.

When completely cooled, store in an airtight container for up to 2 days.

SEASIDE FRUIT SOUP

 Makes 4 servings

1 cup nonfat vanilla yogurt

2 tablespoons freshly squeezed orange juice

1 cup sliced fresh strawberries

1 to 2 tablespoons honey

Tiny pinch of ground black pepper

1/2 cup raspberries

1/2 cup blueberries

1 kiwi, sliced

Extra fruit for garnish

Mix all ingredients together in a food processor or blender. Store in a covered container in the refrigerator for up to 8 hours.

To serve, pour equally into 4 cups or bowls and garnish with extra fruit.

GORILLACORN'S BAKED BANANAS

🧁 Makes 6 to 8 servings

2 cups cornflakes

1 teaspoon cinnamon

4 slightly green bananas, peeled and cut in half lengthwise

2 to 3 tablespoons honey

Frozen vanilla yogurt (optional)

Assorted fresh berries (optional)

1/4 cup powdered sugar (optional)

Preheat oven to 350 degrees F. Line a cookie sheet with aluminum foil and spray with nonstick cooking spray. Set aside.

Pour cornflakes and cinnamon into a ziplock bag and seal shut. Put bag in another ziplock bag and seal shut. Lightly crush mixture with your hands. Set aside.

Place bananas on prepared cookie sheet. With a small spatula or pastry brush, coat each banana half with honey on all sides.

Using a fork, pick up a banana slice and put it into the ziplock bag with the corn flake mixture. Seal bag shut and shake to coat. Place coated banana back onto cookie sheet. Repeat until all banana slices have been coated. Sprinkle any leftover cornflake mixture evenly over the tops of bananas.

Bake for 10 minutes; remove from oven. Garnish warm bananas with frozen yogurt, berries, and powdered sugar if desired. Serve immediately.

SEASHELL CANDY

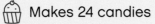

Makes 24 candies

½ pound vanilla candy coating or vanilla almond bark

½ pound candy coating discs in any pastel colors*

Spray 2 (12-shell) madeleine pans** with nonstick cooking spray. Set aside.

Melt each candy coating color in a different pan or container according to package directions. Cool for 2 to 3 minutes.

Put about 1 teaspoon vanilla candy coating into each mold. Spoon about 1 teaspoon colored candy coating on top of the vanilla and swirl with a Popsicle stick or toothpick.

Place pans in the refrigerator for 30 minutes. To remove candy from madeleine pans, turn over and tap on countertop. Any shells that remain in the pan may be carefully taken out by your adult assistant using the point of a sharp knife. Store candy shells covered in a cool place until ready to serve.

*These can be found at any craft store that carries Wilton products.

**Madeleine pans have tiny molds that are shaped like seashells and may be found at gourmet gift stores or baking supply stores.

BITSY BACON AND CHEESE ROLLS

 Makes 16 rolls

1 (8-count) can refrigerated crescent rolls

2 tablespoons flour for work area

6 slices bacon, chopped, cooked, and drained

1 cup grated mozzarella or Swiss cheese

Preheat oven to 375 degrees F. Line a cookie sheet with aluminum foil and spray with nonstick cooking spray.

Remove crescent rolls from can and lay on a flat surface that has been lightly dusted with flour. Turn over each crescent roll to coat both sides with flour.

Cut each crescent roll in half lengthwise to make 2 long, thin triangles.

Place approximately $1/2$ teaspoon bacon bits and $1/2$ teaspoon grated cheese on the widest portion of each triangle. Roll up each crescent roll jellyroll style, starting at the widest end. Place rolls seam side down on prepared cookie sheet about 1 inch apart.

Bake for 10 to 12 minutes, or until golden brown. Remove from oven. Cool 5 minutes on pan and serve.

PINK-AND-WHITE STAR BITES

Makes 8 bites

1 (8-count) can refrigerated biscuits

2 tablespoons flour for work area

8 small slices mozzarella cheese

8 small slices deli ham

1 tablespoon mustard

Preheat oven to 350 degrees F. Line a cookie sheet with aluminum foil and spray with nonstick cooking spray.

Remove biscuits from can and place onto a floured surface. Turn biscuits to coat each side lightly with flour. Cut each biscuit into a star shape with a small cookie cutter.

Use a slightly smaller cookie cutter to cut cheese and ham into star shapes. Spread each biscuit with mustard and top with ham and cheese stars.

Place on prepared cookie sheet and bake for 10 to 12 minutes, or until bottom edges are lightly browned. Remove from oven and let cool on pan for 5 minutes. Serve warm or at room temperature.

UNICORN CALZONES

Makes 8 calzones

1 (8-count) can refrigerated crescent rolls

2 tablespoons flour for work area

2 tablespoons butter, softened

8 thin slices of deli ham or turkey

4 sticks string cheese, cut into 4 pieces

Poppy seeds, optional

Preheat oven to 375 degrees F.

Separate and unroll each crescent roll on a lightly floured work area. Turn to coat each side of roll.

Spread $1/2$ teaspoon of softened butter on each piece of dough, top with 1 slice of ham or turkey, and finish with 2 small chunks of string cheese.

Roll up dough from the widest side and form into a straight horn shape.

Place each horn 2 inches apart on an aluminum foil–lined cookie sheet sprayed with nonstick cooking spray. Sprinkle poppy seeds on top, if using.

Bake 12 to 15 minutes until golden brown and puffy. Remove from oven, cool 5 minutes, and serve hot from the oven or at room temperature.

SNAKICORN'S LOOP-DE-LOOP PRETZELS

Makes 6 pretzel rings

2 tablespoons flour for work area

12 frozen dough dinner rolls, thawed

Assorted liquid food coloring

Water

Q-tips

Kosher salt, optional

Cinnamon and sugar, optional

Preheat oven to 375 degrees F.

Lightly dust work area with flour and spray your hands with nonstick cooking spray. Take each unbaked dinner roll and turn it over in the flour to lightly coat each side. Roll dough back and forth between the palms of your hands to form each roll into a snake shape.

To make a pretzel ring, take 1 snake-shaped piece of dough and link the ends together to form a ring. Then take a second piece of dough and thread it through the ring. Hook the ends of the second piece of dough together. Now you have 2 linked rings, kind of like a paper chain. Repeat these steps until you have 6 pretzel rings.

Place pretzel rings 2 inches apart on a foil-lined cookie sheet that has been sprayed with nonstick cooking spray.

Put several drops of different food coloring in several small bowls and mix each with 1/2 teaspoon water. Using a Q-tip like a paintbrush, decorate each pretzel ring with assorted colors.

You may sprinkle each pretzel ring with kosher salt or a blend of cinnamon and sugar if desired.

Bake for 15 to 20 minutes until lightly browned. Remove from oven, cool 5 minutes, and serve.

GOATICORN'S BREAKFAST QUICHES

🧁 Makes 10 to 12 quiches

1 (17.3 ounce) package
    refrigerated piecrusts

1/2 cup grated Swiss cheese

2 eggs

1/2 teaspoon salt

1/8 teaspoon pepper

2 tablespoons heavy cream

5 to 6 cherry tomatoes,
    sliced

Preheat oven to 400 degrees F.

Generously spray a mini muffin pan with nonstick cooking spray. Cut out the piecrusts with a 2- to 3-inch circle or flower-shaped cookie cutter. Place each cutout inside a muffin cup.

Place approximately 1 teaspoon grated Swiss cheese into the bottom of each pastry shell.

In a medium-size bowl, combine eggs, salt, pepper, and cream. Pour into pastry shells, filling each almost to the top.

Sprinkle with 1 teaspoon grated Swiss cheese and bake for 10 to 12 minutes or until golden brown and slightly puffed. Remove from oven and cool 5 minutes before removing each quiche from pan. Garnish with a cherry tomato slice.

GOLDEN CHEESE BITES

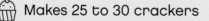

🧁 Makes 25 to 30 crackers

2 cups grated cheddar cheese

1 cup butter, softened

2 cups flour

2 cups crispy rice cereal

$1/2$ teaspoon salt

$1/2$ teaspoon Worcestershire sauce

$1/4$ teaspoon garlic powder

$1/4$ teaspoon cayenne pepper

$1/4$ teaspoon black pepper

2 tablespoons milk

2 tablespoons sesame or poppy seeds

Preheat oven to 350 degrees F. Line 2 cookie sheets with aluminum foil and spray with nonstick cooking spray. Set aside.

In a large bowl, combine cheese, butter, flour, cereal, salt, Worcestershire sauce, garlic powder, cayenne pepper, and black pepper.

Mix well with clean hands and form dough into small $1/2$-inch balls.

Place dough balls 1 inch apart on prepared cookie sheets. Flatten out each ball with your fingertips.

Lightly brush the top of each flattened ball with milk and sprinkle evenly with sesame or poppy seeds.

Bake for 10 to 12 minutes, or until very lightly browned around the outer edges. Carefully put on a cooling rack to cool. Store covered for up to 2 days or freeze for up to 1 month.

COWICORN MILK

 Makes 2 servings

1 cup reduced-fat milk, soy milk, or chocolate milk

1/2 cup fresh or frozen fruit (peaches, bananas, strawberries, blueberries, or raspberries)

1/2 teaspoon vanilla extract or 1/4 teaspoon almond extract

1/2 teaspoon sugar

Dash of cinnamon or nutmeg

Combine milk, fruit, and vanilla or almond extract in blender. Add sugar and cinnamon or nutmeg to taste.

Pour into a glass, add a straw, and drink it up!

TIP: Try chocolate milk with banana, vanilla, and cinnamon. Try regular milk with peaches, almond extract, and nutmeg. Try soy milk with strawberries and cinnamon.

LEMONADE FLOATS

 Makes 4 servings

1 cup fresh lemon juice (about 10 to 12 lemons, squeezed)

$1/2$ cup honey or to taste

$1/2$ teaspoon vanilla extract

$1/2$ cup warm water

3 cups chilled sparkling water or club soda

Assorted fruit sorbets (lemon, lime, orange, raspberry, strawberry, and/or blueberry)

Fresh fruit for garnish

Combine lemon juice, honey, vanilla, and water in mixing bowl. Whisk to blend ingredients.

Pour lemon juice mixture into a large pitcher and add chilled sparkling water or club soda, whisking to combine. Set pitcher in freezer for 5 minutes to cool quickly. Don't forget and leave it there!

While lemonade is chilling, choose your flavor—or combination of flavors—of sorbet. Using a melon baller, scoop 4 to 6 mini sorbet balls per serving. Place them inside each glass and pour sparkling lemonade on top.

Garnish with fresh fruit and a straw.

CAMELCORN'S SWEET CHAI TEA

🧁 Makes 4 to 5 servings

4 cups filtered water

3 regular tea bags (English breakfast tea, orange pekoe, Darjeeling, or Earl Grey)

2 cinnamon sticks

6 cardamom seeds

3 whole cloves

6 black peppercorns

$1/4$ teaspoon freshly grated nutmeg

$1/2$ inch thinly sliced fresh ginger

1 cup plain or vanilla soy milk

4 teaspoons honey or maple syrup

Place water, tea bags, and all spices in a large saucepan over medium heat and bring to a boil. Reduce heat and simmer 10 to 15 minutes.

Remove from heat and add soy milk. Return to heat and simmer another 5 minutes, or until steaming. Remove from heat.

Pour chai through a large strainer into a teapot. Stir in honey or maple syrup and serve. Chai may also be covered and refrigerated for up to 1 day and then served cold over crushed ice.

PERFECT PINK LEMONADE

Makes 15 servings

2 liters flavored sparkling water (strawberry, raspberry, or lemon), chilled

$1/2$ cup grenadine syrup

Juice of 8 to 10 lemons

$1/2$ cup sugar (or more to taste)

Crushed ice (optional)

Pink or purple sugar crystals (optional)

Combine chilled flavored sparkling water, grenadine, lemon juice, and sugar. Stir with a metal whisk to blend ingredients. Add crushed ice if desired.

If desired, moisten rim of small punch cups or fancy juice glasses and dip in pink or purple sugar crystals. Pour lemonade immediately into cups or glasses and serve.

COOL BREEZE SLUSHIES

🧁 Makes 4 servings

3 cups fresh watermelon
    cubes

1 cup crushed ice

4 teaspoons lime juice

1 cup raspberry sorbet

Granny Smith apple cubes
    for garnish

In a blender, combine watermelon, ice, and lime juice. Add raspberry sorbet by the spoonful and blend until smooth.

Divide mixture equally between glass punch cups or glasses.

Garnish with apples and serve immediately.

SWIRLED SMOOTHIES

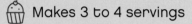

🧁 Makes 3 to 4 servings

Cherry

$1/2$ cup vanilla yogurt

$1/2$ banana

$1/2$ cup vanilla soy milk

1 cup pitted fresh cherries
(frozen may be used)

Orange

$1/2$ cup vanilla yogurt

$1/2$ banana

$1/2$ cup vanilla soy milk

$1/2$ cup fresh squeezed
orange juice

For the cherry smoothie, mix vanilla yogurt, banana, and milk in a blender. Add the cherries and blend on low speed for 30 seconds. Pour smoothie into a small pitcher or pour-spout measuring cup and place in freezer. Rinse out blender and dry.

For the orange smoothie, place all ingredients in blender and blend on low speed for 30 seconds. Pour smoothie into a small pitcher or pour-spout measuring cup.

Pour both smoothies into tall serving glasses at the same time to make them swirl. Serve immediately.

LAA-TEE-DAH PINK LIMEADE

🧁 **Makes 8 servings**

³/₄ cup lime juice

1 cup sugar

2 liters lemon-lime soda, chilled

¹/₂ cup maraschino cherry juice or grenadine syrup

1 teaspoon vanilla extract

3 to 4 cups crushed ice

Garnish

8 maraschino cherries with stems

1 lime, sliced into 8 slices

In a large bowl, combine lime juice and sugar. Stir to blend until sugar is completely dissolved.

Stir in soda, cherry juice or grenadine syrup, and vanilla. Place crushed ice in glasses and pour in limeade. Garnish each serving with a maraschino cherry and lime slice. Serve immediately.

DREAMY CREAMY CHOCOLATE SHAKE

 Makes 2 servings

- 2 cups chocolate frozen yogurt
- 2 tablespoons chocolate syrup
- 1 cup chocolate or vanilla almond milk
- $1/2$ teaspoon vanilla extract

Garnish

- $1/2$ cup whipped cream or whipped topping
- 2 teaspoons chocolate sprinkles
- 2 maraschino cherries with stems

Combine frozen yogurt, chocolate syrup, and almond milk in a blender. Blend until smooth.

Add vanilla and blend again.

Pour shakes into glasses. Top each shake with whipped cream, chocolate sprinkles, and a maraschino cherry.

FROZEN PEPPERMINT HOT CHOCOLATE

 Makes 8 servings

Frozen Peppermint Whipped Topping

1 (4-ounce) container frozen whipped topping, thawed

10 to 12 hard peppermint candies, crushed

1 to 2 drops red food coloring

Extra hard peppermint candies for garnish

Hot Chocolate

4 cups whole or reduced-fat milk

Pinch of salt

$1^1/_2$ cups milk chocolate or semisweet chocolate chips

1 teaspoon vanilla extract

Line a cookie sheet with aluminum foil or waxed paper. Set aside.

In a large mixing bowl, combine the whipped topping with crushed peppermints. Add 1 to 2 drops red food coloring and stir to blend.

Drop 8 teaspoons of whipped topping in the shape of dollops, about $1^1/_2$ to 2 inches in diameter, on the prepared cookie sheet. Place cookie sheet in the freezer and freeze until firm, about 20 to 30 minutes.

Heat milk and salt in a large saucepan over medium heat until steaming. Remove from heat and add chocolate chips. Return to low heat and whisk until chocolate chips are melted and mixture is smooth. Remove hot chocolate from heat and add vanilla.

Carefully ladle into teacups or small mugs. Garnish each drink with a dollop of frozen peppermint whipped topping and a hard candy.

INDEX

DID YOU KNOW the Llamacorn loves to share the cookies he makes? Learn about his kindness and his friends in *The Llamacorn Is Kind* (picture book and board book) and *Llamacorn Saves the Day*!

THE LLAMACORN IS KIND
978-1-4236-5262-5 (picture book)
978-1-4236-5438-4 (board book)

LLAMACORN SAVES THE DAY
978-1-4236-5439-1

ABOUT THE AUTHOR

Barbara Beery founded Batter Up Kids in 1991, and has since taught thousands of children the joy of cooking through year-round classes, cooking birthday parties, and summer cooking camps. She has written 12 cookbooks, appeared twice on the *Today Show, CBN* with Pat Robertson, and her business has been featured in the *New York Times* and *Entrepreneur Magazine,* as well as dozens of other local and national publications. She is currently working closely with and has the endorsement of Rachael Ray's Yum-o Organization, Susan G. Komen, American Heart Association, and the Great American Bake Sale. She lives in Austin, TX.

METRIC CONVERSION CHART

VOLUME MEASUREMENTS		WEIGHT MEASUREMENTS		TEMPERATURE CONVERSION	
U.S.	METRIC	U.S.	METRIC	FAHRENHEIT	CELSIUS
1 teaspoon	5 ml	1/2 ounce	15 g	250	120
1 tablespoon	15 ml	1 ounce	30 g	300	150
1/4 cup	60 ml	3 ounces	90 g	325	160
1/3 cup	75 ml	4 ounces	115 g	350	180
1/2 cup	125 ml	8 ounces	225 g	375	190
2/3 cup	150 ml	12 ounces	350 g	400	200
3/4 cup	175 ml	1 pound	450 g	425	220
1 cup	250 ml	2 1/4 pounds	1 kg	450	230